HAL•LEONARD
ESSENTIAL SONGS

PIANO VOCAL GUITAR

Wedding

ISBN 978-1-4234-0929-8

HAL•LEONARD®
CORPORATION
7777 W. BLUEMOUND RD. P.O. BOX 13819 MILWAUKEE, WI 53213

Visit Hal Leonard Online at
www.halleonard.com

CONTENTS

ALL I ASK OF YOU
from THE PHANTOM OF THE OPERA

Music by ANDREW LLOYD WEBBER
Lyrics by CHARLES HART
Additional Lyrics by RICHARD STILGOE

No more talk of dark-ness, for-get these wide-eyed fears: I'm

here, noth-ing can harm you, my words will warm and calm you.

Let me be your free-dom, let day-light dry your tears: I'm

AMAZED

Words and Music by MARV GREEN,
CHRIS LINDSEY and AIMEE MAYO

Moderately slow Country Ballad

With pedal

Ev -'ry time our eyes meet, this feel -in' in - side me
The smell of your skin, the taste of your kiss,

is al - most more than I can take.
the way you whis per in the dark.

*Recorded a half step lower.

ALL THE THINGS YOU ARE

from VERY WARM FOR MAY

Lyrics by OSCAR HAMMERSTEIN II
Music by JEROME KERN

ALWAYS AND FOREVER

Words and Music by
ROD TEMPERTON

AMEN KIND OF LOVE

Words and Music by TREY BRUCE
and WAYNE TESTER

AVE MARIA

By FRANZ SCHUBERT

Sehr langsam (Molto adagio)

pp

(With pedal)

A - ve Ma - ri - a!
A - ve Ma - ri - a!

a! gra - ti - a ple -
a! Ma - ter De -

A - ve Ma - ri - -
A - ve Ma - ri - -

a!
a!

sim.

dim.

BACK AT ONE

Words and Music by
BRIAN McKNIGHT

Slowly

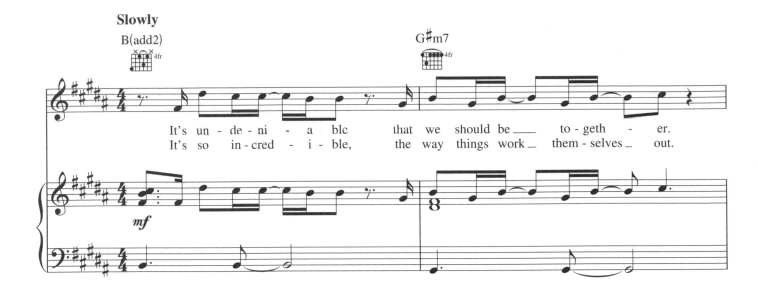

It's un-de-ni-a-ble that we should be __ to-geth-er.
It's so in-cred-i-ble, the way things work __ them-selves __ out.

It's un-be-liev-a-ble how I used to say __ that I'd __ fall nev-er.
And all e-mo-tion-al, once you know what __ it's all __ a-bout, __ hey.

The ba-sis is need to know. If you don't know just how I feel, __ then
And un-de-sir-a-ble, for us to be a-part.

34

BEAUTIFUL

Words and Music by JIM BRICKMAN,
JACK KUGELL and JAMIE JONES

Moderately slow

With pedal

From the mo-ment I saw___ you, from the mo-ment I looked___ in-to___ your eyes,___
Hold-ing you___ in my___ arms, no one else___ -'s fit _____ so per - fect-ly.___

___ there was some-thing a - bout ___ you. ___ I knew ___ I ___ knew ___
___ I could dance ___ for-ev - er ___ with you, ___ with ___ you. ___

BEST THING THAT EVER HAPPENED TO ME

Words and Music by
JIM WEATHERLY

BLESS THE BROKEN ROAD

Words and Music by MARCUS HUMMON,
BOBBY BOYD and JEFF HANNA

D.S. al Coda

BRIDAL CHORUS
from LOHENGRIN

By RICHARD WAGNER

Moderato

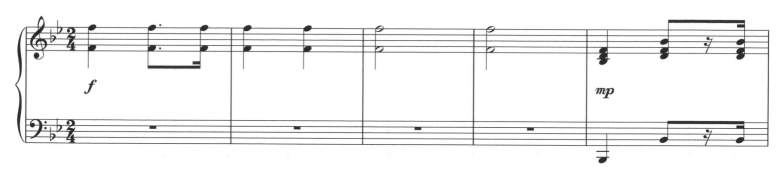

BUTTERFLY KISSES

Words and Music by BOB CARLISLE
and RANDY THOMAS

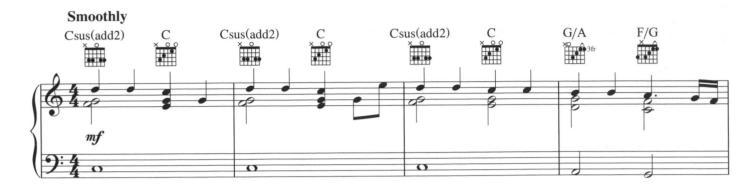

There's two things I know for sure. _____ She was
Sweet six - teen to - day, _____
She'll change her name to - day. _____

sent here from heav - en and she's dad-dy's lit - tle girl. _____ As I
look - ing like her mom - ma a lit - tle more ev - 'ry day. _____
She'll make a prom - ise, and I'll give her _____ a - way. _____

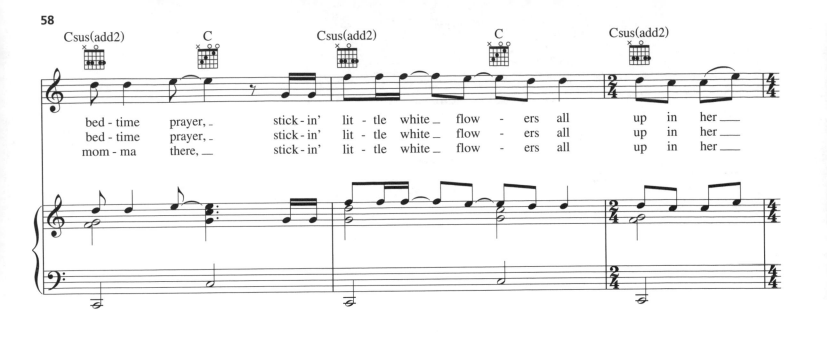

bed - time   prayer, _   stick - in'   lit - tle   white _   flow -   ers   all   up   in   her ___
bed - time   prayer, _   stick - in'   lit - tle   white _   flow -   ers   all   up   in   her ___
mom - ma   there, _   stick - in'   lit - tle   white _   flow -   ers   all   up   in   her ___

hair.
hair.   "You   know   how   much _   I   love _   you, Dad -   dy,   but   if
hair.   "Walk   me   down _   the   aisle, _   Dad -   dy,   it's
"Walk   be - side _   the   po -   ny,   Dad -   dy,   it's

my   first   ride. ___   I   know   the   cake _   looks   fun -   ny,   Dad -   dy,   but
you   don't   mind, _   I'm   on - ly   goin' _   to   kiss _   you   on _   the
just   a - bout   time.   Does   my   wed - ding   gown _   look   pret -   ty,   Dad -   dy?   Dad -

CAN'T HELP FALLING IN LOVE

from the Paramount Picture BLUE HAWAII

Words and Music by GEORGE DAVID WEISS,
HUGO PERETTI and LUIGI CREATORE

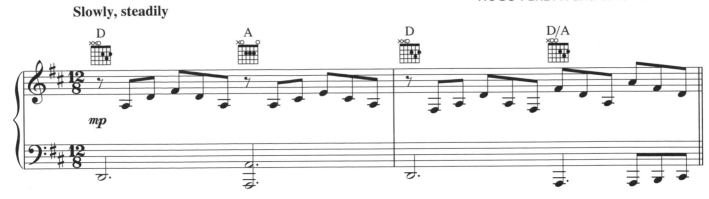

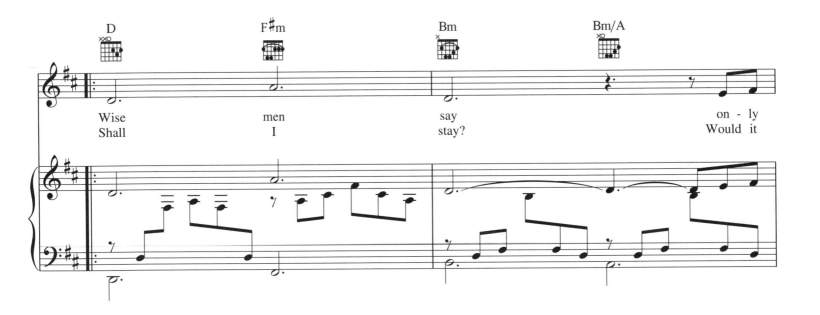

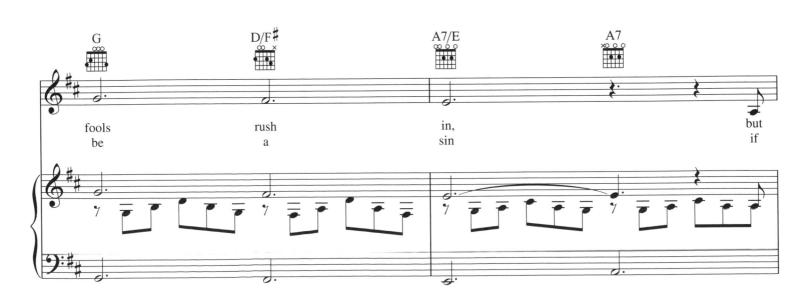

F#m   B7   Em   A7

some things __ are __ meant to be.

D   F#m   Bm

Take my hand, take my

G   D/F#   A7/E   A7

whole life too, for

G   A   Bm   G6   Em

I can't help fall - ing __ in

CANON IN D

By JOHANN PACHELBEL

Adagio

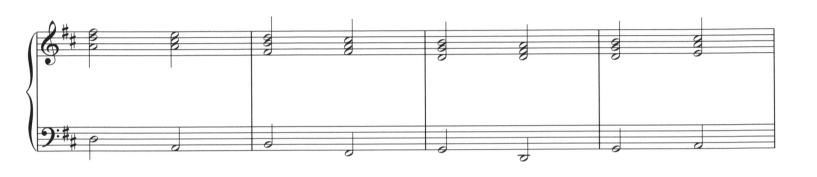

rit.

COULD I HAVE THIS DANCE

Words and Music by WAYLAND HOLYFIELD
and BOB HOUSE

Moderately

I'll al - ways re - mem - ber the song they were
al - ways re - mem - ber that mag - ic

play - ing, the first time we danced and I knew.
mo - ment, when I held you close to me.

As we swayed to the mu - sic and held to each
As we moved to - geth - er, I knew each for -

DON'T KNOW MUCH

Words and Music by BARRY MANN,
CYNTHIA WEIL and TOM SNOW

ENDLESS LOVE

from ENDLESS LOVE

Words and Music by
LIONEL RICHIE

Oh, _____ and _ love, _____

cresc.

mf

(Everything I Do)
I DO IT FOR YOU
from the Motion Picture ROBIN HOOD: PRINCE OF THIEVES

Words and Music by BRYAN ADAMS,
ROBERT JOHN LANGE and MICHAEL KAMEN

FOREVER AND EVER, AMEN

Words and Music by PAUL OVERSTREET
and DON SCHLITZ

FOREVER AND FOR ALWAYS

Words and Music by SHANIA TWAIN
and R.J. LANGE

Moderately

Oh, _____ I can hear your heart _ beat now. _ I can hear it beat - ing loud. _

In your arms _____
In your heart _____
I can still feel the way you want _ me when you
I can still hear a beat for ev - 'ry time you

* *Recorded a half step lower.*

In your eyes _____ I can

still see the look of the one __ who real-ly loves me. _____ The one who

would-n't put an - y-thing else __ in the world a - bove me. _____ I can

C
D
Am
G
sweet face.
I'm keep-ing you for-ev-er and for al-ways.
G/B
Em
C
Ahh,
D
G
Em
I'm keep-ing you for-ev-er.
But you keep me wait-ing,
ahh,
C
D
G
umm, here for-ev-er
in your arms.

FROM THIS MOMENT ON

Words and Music by SHANIA TWAIN
and R.J. LANGE

Female (Spoken): I do swear that I'll al - ways be there. _

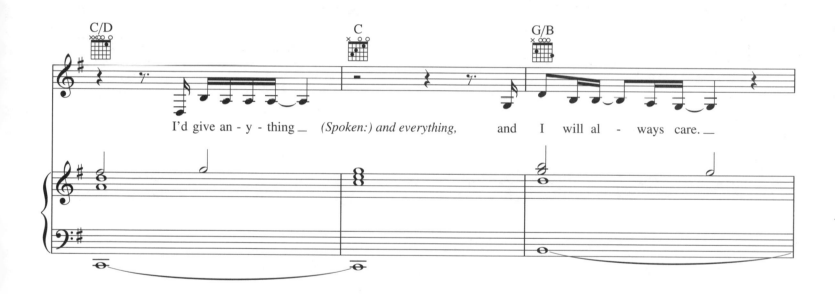

I'd give an - y - thing _ (Spoken:) and everything, and I will al - ways care. _

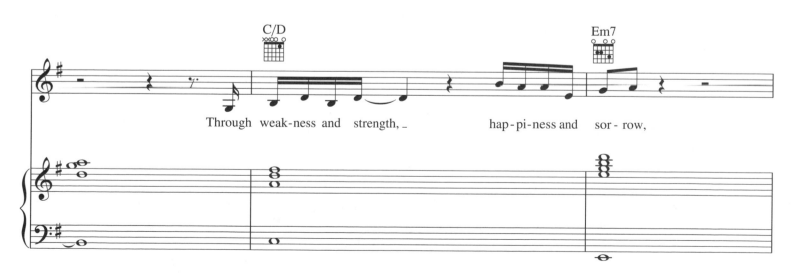

Through weak - ness and strength, _ hap - pi - ness and sor - row,

106

*Male vocals sung an octave higher throughout.

FOREVER I DO
(The Wedding Song)

Words and Music by CYNTHIA BIGGS
and DEXTER WANSEL

115

GABRIEL'S OBOE
from the Motion Picture THE MISSION

Words and Music by
ENNIO MORRICONE

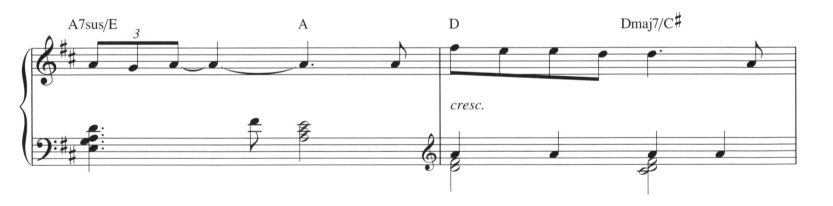

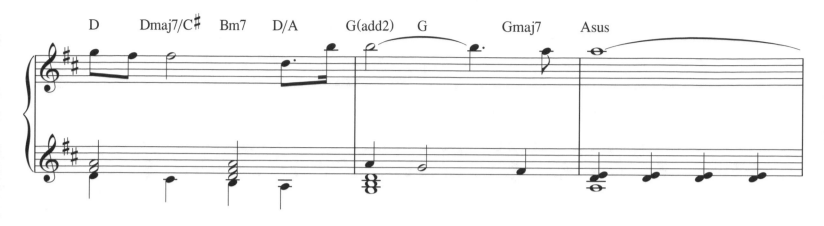

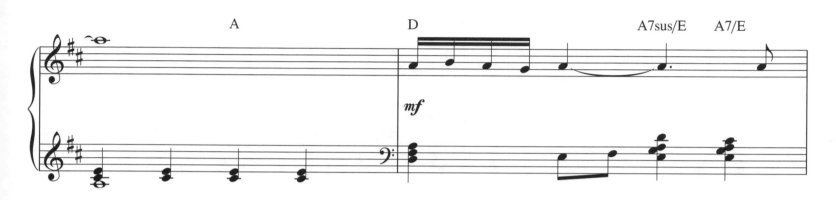

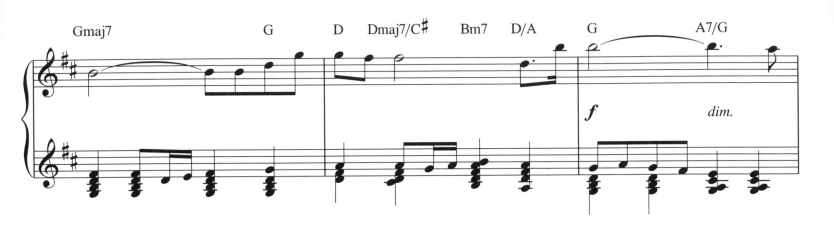

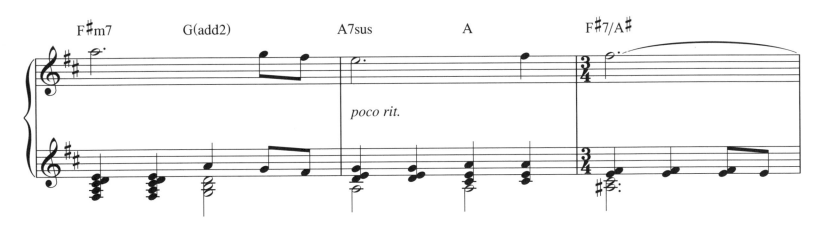

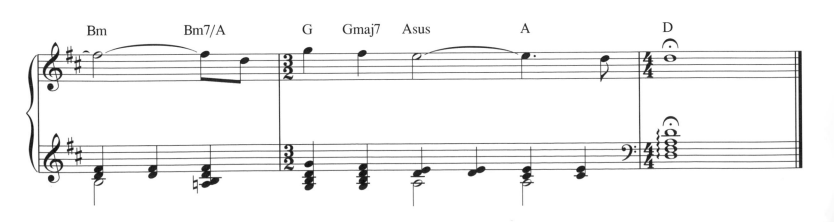

GROW OLD WITH ME

Words and Music by
JOHN LENNON

HALLELUJAH

Words and Music by
LEONARD COHEN

Moderately slow, in 2

1. I've heard there was a se-cret chord ___ that
2.-5. *See additional lyrics*

Da-vid played, ___ and it pleased the Lord, ___ but you don't ___ real-ly

care for mu-sic, ___ do you? ___

It

lu - jah. _____ Hal - le - lu

jah. _____

rit.

Additional Lyrics

2. Your faith was strong, but you needed proof.
   You saw her bathing on the roof.
   Her beauty and the moonlight overthrew you.
   She tied you to a kitchen chair.
   She broke your throne; she cut your hair.
   And from your lips she drew the Hallelujah. *(To Chorus)*

3. Maybe I have been here before.
   I know this room; I've walked this floor.
   I used to live alone before I knew you.
   I've seen your flag on the marble arch.
   Love is not a victory march.
   It's a cold and it's a broken Hallelujah. *(To Chorus)*

4. There was a time you let me know
   What's real and going on below.
   But now you never show it to me, do you?
   And remember when I moved in you,
   The holy dark was movin' too,
   And every breath we drew was Hallelujah. *(To Chorus)*

5. Maybe there's a God above,
   And all I ever learned from love
   Was how to shoot at someone who outdrew you.
   And it's not a cry you can hear at night.
   It's not somebody who's seen the light.
   It's a cold and it's a broken Hallelujah. *(To Chorus)*

HAVE I TOLD YOU LATELY

Words and Music by
VAN MORRISON

Slowly, with expression

Have I told ___ you late-ly that I love you?   Have I

told you there's no one else ___ a-bove ___ you?

Fill my heart ___ with glad - ness,   take a - way all ___ my sad - ness,

HOUSEHOLD OF FAITH

Words by BRENT LAMB
Music by JOHN ROSASCO

With warmth

Here we are ___ at the start, ___ com-mit-ting to ___ each
Now to be ___ a fam-i-ly ___ we've got to love ___ each

oth-er ___ by His Word and from our hearts,
oth-er at an-y cost un-self-ish-ly;

HERE AND NOW

Words and Music by TERRY STEELE
and DAVID ELLIOT

HERE, THERE AND EVERYWHERE

Words and Music by JOHN LENNON
and PAUL McCARTNEY

141

HOW BEAUTIFUL

Words and Music by
TWILA PARIS

beau - ti - ful _____ the hands _____ that _____ served _____ the
beau - ti - ful _____ the heart _____ that _____ bled, _____ that
beau - ti - ful _____ the ra - diant _ Bride _____ who

wine and the bread ___ and the sons ___ of the earth. How ___
took all my ___ sin and ___ bore it in - stead. How ___
waits for her ___ Groom with His light ___ in her eyes. How ___

I BELIEVE IN YOU AND ME

from the Touchstone Motion Picture THE PREACHER'S WIFE

Words and Music by DAVID WOLFERT
and SANDY LINZER

153

I FINALLY FOUND SOMEONE

from THE MIRROR HAS TWO FACES

Words and Music by BARBRA STREISAND,
MARVIN HAMLISCH, ROBERT LANGE
and BRYAN ADAMS

Male: I fi-n'lly found some-one who knocks me off my feet.

I fi-n'lly found the one ___ that makes me feel com-plete.

Female: It start-ed o-ver cof-fee. We start-ed out as friends.

I DO
(Cherish You)

Words and Music by ROBERT STE
and DAN

I DO
(Cherish You)

Words and Music by ROBERT STEGALL
and DAN HILL

I HONESTLY LOVE YOU

Words and Music by PETER ALLEN
and JEFF BARRY

May-be I hang a-round __ here a lit-tle more than I should; we

You don't __ have to an - swer; I see it in your eyes.

both know I got some - where else __ to go. But

May-be it was bet - ter left __ un - said. But

I SWEAR

Words and Music by FRANK MYERS
and GARY BAKER

I see the ques - tions in___ your eyes;___   I know what's weigh -
I'll give you ev - 'ry - thing___ I can;___   I'll build your dreams __

I PLEDGE MY LOVE

Words by DINO FEKARIS
Music by DINO FEKARIS and FREDDIE PERREN

I WILL BE HERE

Words and Music by
STEVEN CURTIS CHAPMAN

IF

Words and Music by
DAVID GATES

IN MY LIFE

Words and Music by JOHN LENNON
and PAUL McCARTNEY

THE IRISH WEDDING SONG

Words and Music by
IAN BETTERIDGE

Moderate, gentle Waltz

(T)Here they stand, hand in hand, they've ex-changed wed-ding
May they find peace of mind comes to all who are
As they go, may they know ev-'ry love that was

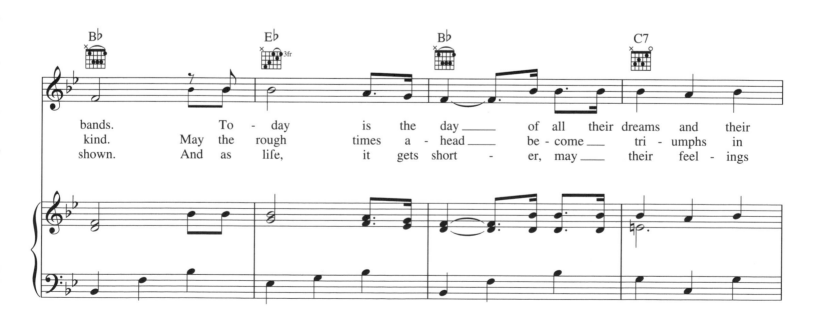

bands. To - day is the day of all their dreams and their
kind. May the rough times a - head be-come tri - umphs in
shown. And as life, it gets short - er, may their feel - ings

JESU, JOY OF MAN'S DESIRING

By JOHANN SEBASTIAN BACH

203

THE KEEPER OF THE STARS

Words and Music by KAREN STALEY,
DANNY MAYO and DICKEY LEE

LARGO
from XERXES

By GEORGE FRIDERIC HANDEL

Larghetto

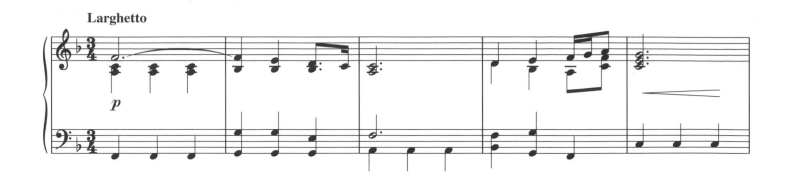

LET IT BE ME
(Je T'appartiens)

English Words by MANN CURTIS
French Words by PIERRE DeLANOE
Music by GILBERT BECAUD

Relaxed

I bless the day I found you,
If, for each day bit of glad - ness,

I want to stay a - round you, and so I
some - one must stay taste of sad - ness, I'll bear the

beg you, let it be me.
sor - row, let it be me.

NEVER MY LOVE

Words and Music by DON ADDRISI
and DICK ADDRISI

LONGER

Words and Music by
DAN FOGELBERG

LOVE IN ANY LANGUAGE

Words and Music by JOHN MAYS
and JON MOHR

* French   *** Russian (phonetic)
** Spanish   **** Hebrew

LOVE ME TENDER

Words and Music by ELVIS PRESLEY
and VERA MATSON

Moderately slow

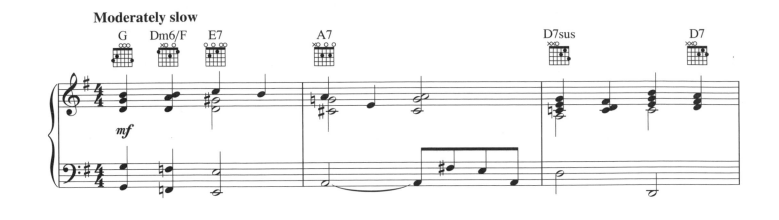

Love me ten - der, love me sweet,
Love me ten - der, love me long,
Love me ten - der, love me dear,
When at last my dreams come true,

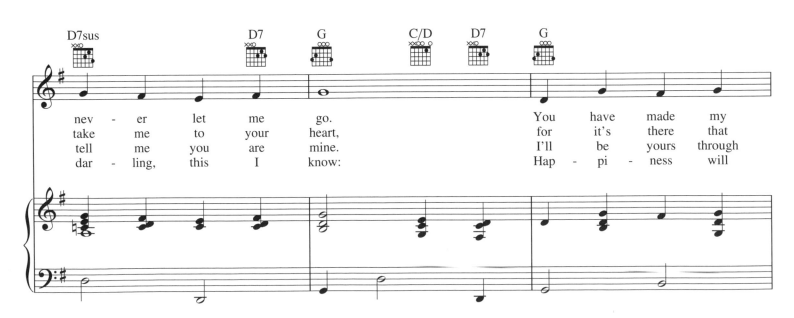

nev - er let me go.
take me to your heart,
tell me you are mine.
dar - ling, this I know:

You have made my
for it's made there that
I'll be yours through
Hap - pi - ness will

LOVE WILL KEEP US ALIVE

Words and Music by PETER VALE,
JIM CAPALDI and PAUL CARRACK

MORE THAN WORDS

Words and Music by NUNO BETTENCOURT
and GARY CHERONE

Moderately slow

Say-in' "I ___ love ___ you" is
Now that I've ___ tried ___ to

not the words ___ I want ___ to ___ hear ___ from you. ___ It's not that I ___
talk to you ___ and make ___ you ___ un - der - stand, ___ all ___ you ___

* *Recorded a half step lower.*

G
Em
G/B
Em11
5fr
G/B
-n't have to say that you love me 'cause
Am7
D7
G
G/B
G
G/B
I'd al - read - y know. What would you do
D/F♯
Em
G/B
Bm7
C
if my heart was torn in two? More than words
Am
D7
G
to show you feel that your love for me is real.

MY HEART WILL GO ON
(Love Theme from 'Titanic')
from the Paramount and Twentieth Century Fox Motion Picture TITANIC

Music by JAMES HORNER
Lyric by WILL JENNINGS

NOBODY LOVES ME LIKE YOU DO

Words by PAMELA PHILLIPS
Music by JAMES P. DUNNE

Female: Like a can - dle burn - ing bright,

love is glow - ing in ___ your eyes. ___

ON BENDED KNEE

Words and Music by JAMES HARRIS III
and TERRY LEWIS

Slowly, with motion

Dar-lin', I, I can't ex-plain. ___
So man-y nights I dream of you ___
(Spoken:) Baby, I'm sorry. Please forgive me for all the wrong

ONE IN A MILLION YOU

Words and Music by
SAM DEES

Love had played its games on me so long ____ I start-ed to ____ be-lieve ____ I'd nev-er find ____ an-y-one. ____ Doubt had tried ____

PERFECT MOMENT

Words and Music by JIM MARR
and WENDY PAGE

Moderately slow

Recorded a half step lower.

THE POWER OF LOVE

Words by MARY SUSAN APPLEGATE and JENNIFER RUSH
Music by CANDY DEROUGE and GUNTHER MENDE

Slowly, with a steady beat

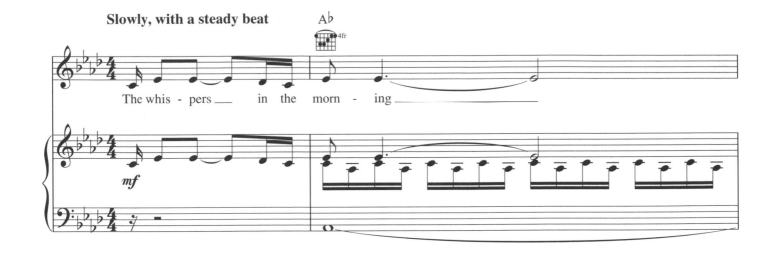

The whis - pers ___ in the morn - ing ___

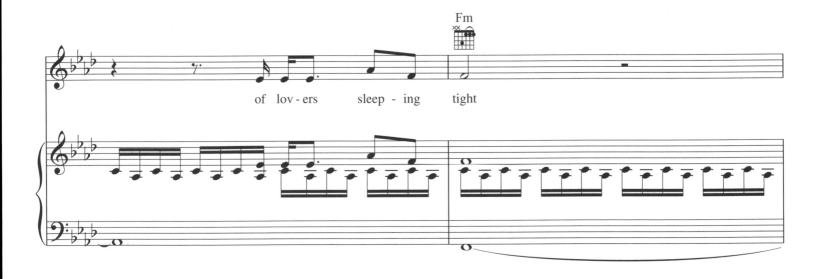

of lov - ers sleep - ing tight

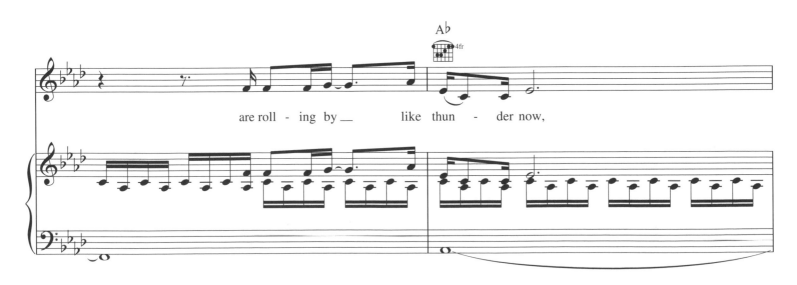

are roll - ing by ___ like thun - der now,

D♭
E♭
The sound of your heart
A♭
D♭
E♭
beat - ing made it clear sud-den -
Fm
D♭
E♭
A♭
ly. The feel-ing that I can't go on
D♭
E♭
D♭
E♭
D♭
E♭
D.S. al Coda
(take 2nd ending)
is light-years a - way. 'Cause I'm your la -

THE PROMISE
(I'll Never Say Goodbye)
Theme from the Universal Picture THE PROMISE

Words by ALAN and MARILYN BERGMAN
Music by DAVID SHIRE

Cue notes optional 2nd time

SOMEWHERE OUT THERE

from AN AMERICAN TAIL

Words and Music by JAMES HORNER,
BARRY MANN and CYNTHIA WEIL

through,   then   we'll be to - geth - er some - where out there,   out

where dreams   come   true. _____

SAVE THE BEST FOR LAST

Words and Music by PHIL GALDSTON,
JON LIND and WENDY WALDMAN

SPEND MY LIFE WITH YOU

Words and Music by ERIC BENÉT,
GEORGE NASH and DEMONTE POSEY

STARTING HERE, STARTING NOW

Words by RICHARD MALTBY JR.
Music by DAVID SHIRE

Quite slowly, with a steady beat

SUDDENLY

Words and Music by BILLY OCEAN
and KEITH DIAMOND

1. I used to think that love was just a fair-y tale,
2. (See additional lyrics)

un-til that first hel-lo, un-til that first smile.

Additional Lyrics

2. Girl, you're everything a man could want and more,
One thousand words are not enough
To say what I feel inside.
Holding hands as we walk along the shore
Never felt like this before,
Now you're all I'm living for.
Chorus

SUNRISE, SUNSET

from the Musical FIDDLER ON THE ROOF

Words by SHELDON HARNICK
Music by JERRY BOCK

Moderately slow Waltz tempo

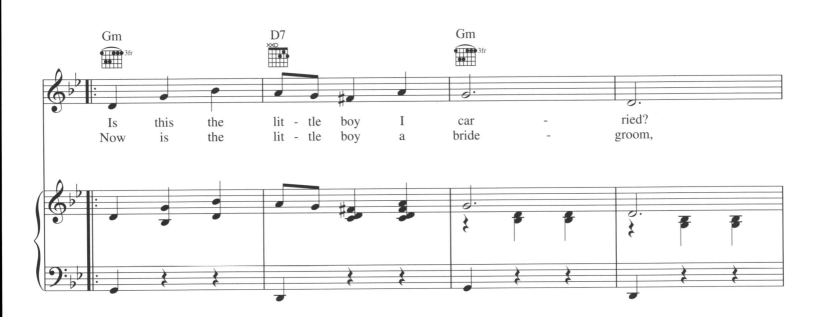

Is this the lit-tle boy I car - ried?
Now is the lit-tle boy a bride - groom,

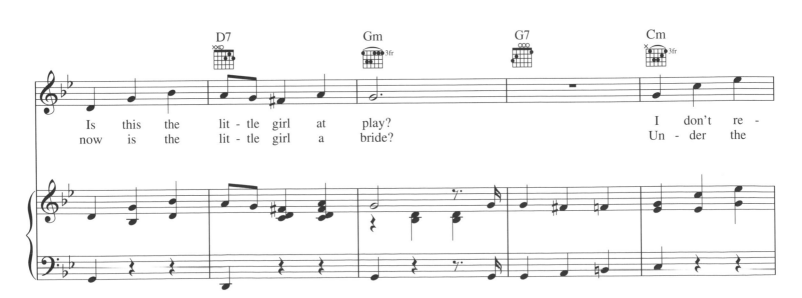

Is this the lit-tle girl at play?
now is the lit-tle girl a bride?

I don't re -
Un - der the

THIS DAY

Words and Music by
LOWELL ALEXANDER

This day is frag - ile.
This day is fleet - ing;
This day is frail. __

Soon it will
When it slips a -
It will pass

end,
way,
by,

and once it has van - ished it will
not all our mon - ey can __
so be - fore it's too late to re -

Recorded a half step higher.

THIS IS THE DAY
(A Wedding Song)

Words and Music by
SCOTT WESLEY BROWN

this is the day, _____

This is the day. _____

8vb

A TIME FOR US
(Love Theme)
from the Paramount Picture ROMEO AND JULIET

Words by LARRY KUSIK and EDDIE SNYDER
Music by NINO ROTA

TONIGHT, I CELEBRATE MY LOVE

Music by MICHAEL MASSER
Lyric by GERRY GOFFIN

Slowly and expressively

To -

night ___ I cel - e - brate my love ___ for you; ___ it seems ___ the nat - u - ral
night ___ I cel - e - brate my love ___ for you; ___ and hope ___ that deep in - side you
night ___ I cel - e - brate my love ___ for you; ___ and soon ___ this old world will

thing ___ to do. To - night ___ no one's gon-na find us, ___ we'll leave the world ___ be -
feel ___ it too. To - night ___ our spir - its will be climb-ing to a sky lit up ___ with
seem ___ brand-new. To - night ___ we will both dis - cov - er ___ how friends turn in - to

TRUE LOVE
from HIGH SOCIETY

Words and Music by
COLE PORTER

TRUMPET VOLUNTARY

By JEREMIAH CLARKE

TRULY

Words and Music by
LIONEL RICHIE

UP WHERE WE BELONG

from the Paramount Picture AN OFFICER AND A GENTLEMAN

Words by WILL JENNINGS
Music by BUFFY SAINTE-MARIE and JACK NITZSCHE

WE'VE ONLY JUST BEGUN

Words and Music by ROGER NICHOLS
and PAUL WILLIAMS

WEDDING PRAYER

Words and Music by
MARY RICE HOPKINS

WEDDING MARCH

By FELIX MENDELSSOHN

Allegro

D.S. al Fine

WHEN I FALL IN LOVE

Words by EDWARD HEYMAN
Music by VICTOR YOUNG

Slowly, with much feeling

YOU AND I

Words and Music by
FRANK MYERS

WHEN YOU SAY NOTHING AT ALL

Words and Music by DON SCHLITZ
and PAUL OVERSTREET

Moderately slow

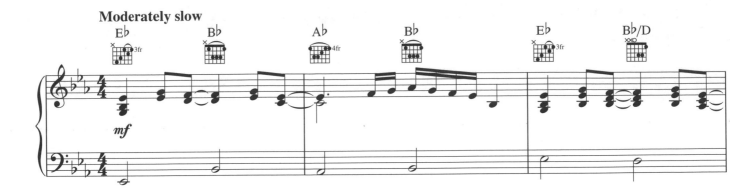

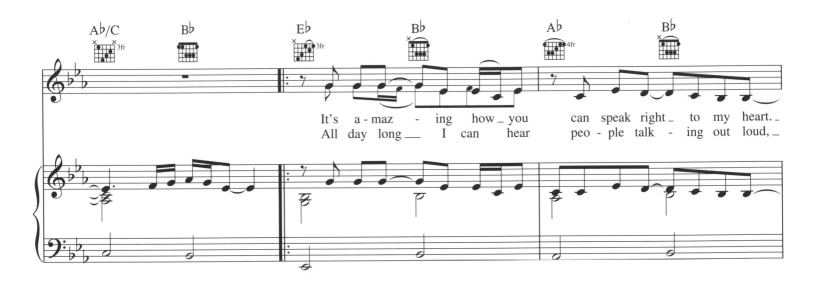

It's a-maz-ing how you can speak right to my heart.
All day long I can hear peo-ple talk-ing out loud,

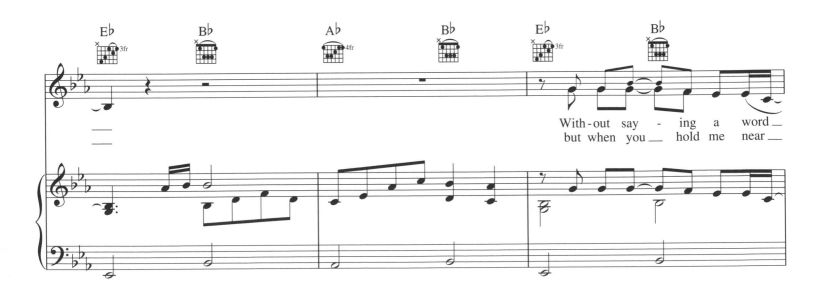

With-out say-ing a word
but when you hold me near

A WHOLE NEW WORLD
(Aladdin's Theme)
from Walt Disney's ALADDIN

Music by ALAN MENKEN
Lyrics by TIM RICE

YOU DECORATED MY LIFE

Words and Music by DEBBI HUPP
and BOB MORRISON

YOU LIGHT UP MY LIFE

Words and Music by
JOSEPH BROOKS

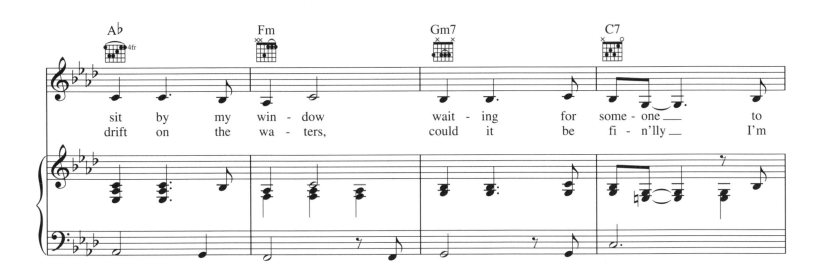

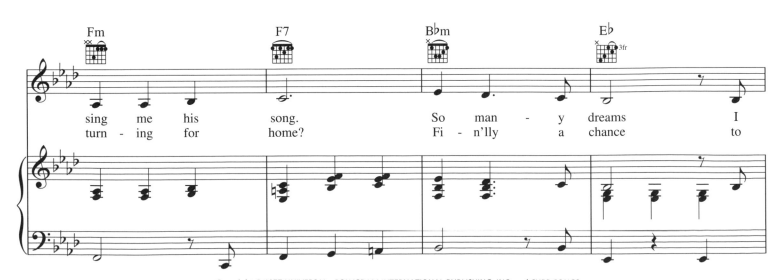

YOU NEEDED ME

Words and Music by
RANDY GOODRUM

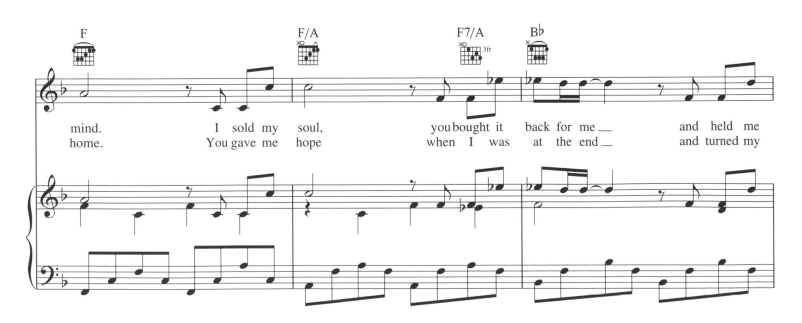

YOU RAISE ME UP

Words and Music by BRENDAN GRAHAM
and ROLF LOVLAND

Moderately slow

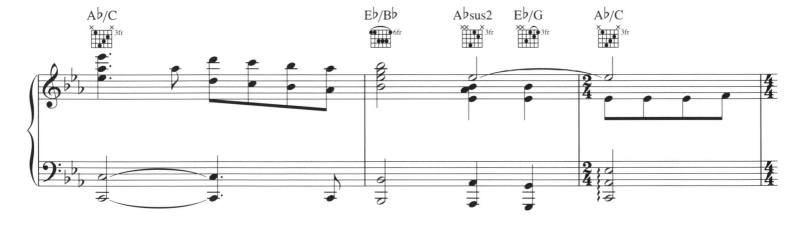

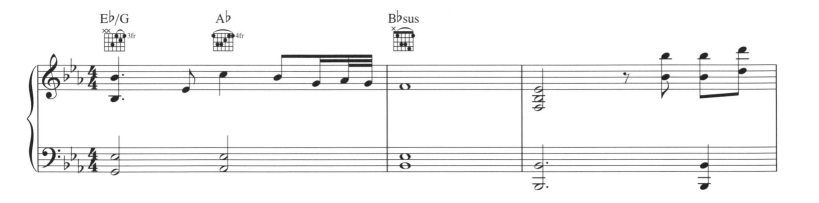

YOU'LL ACCOMP'NY ME

Words and Music by
BOB SEGER

meant to be.   Some-day, la - dy, you'll ac - com - p'ny me. ___
meant to be.   Some-day, la - dy, you'll ac - com - p'ny me. ___

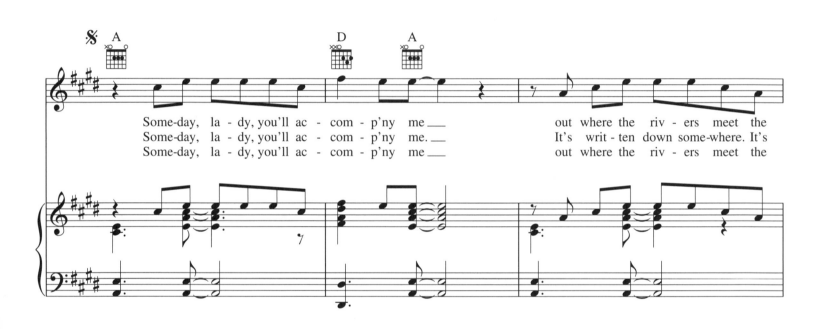

Some-day, la - dy, you'll ac - com - p'ny me ___   out where the riv - ers meet the
Some-day, la - dy, you'll ac - com - p'ny me. ___   It's writ - ten down some-where. It's
Some-day, la - dy, you'll ac - com - p'ny me ___   out where the riv - ers meet the

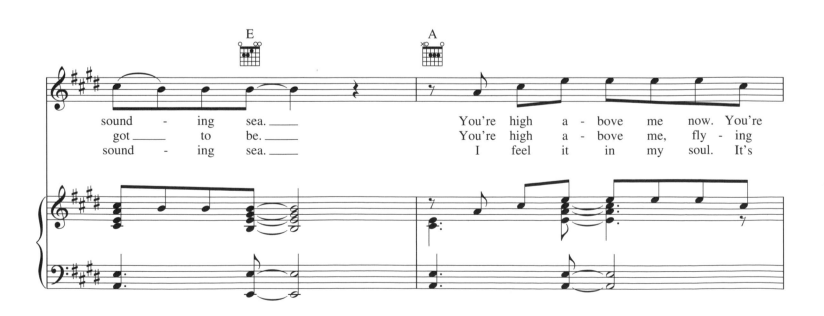

sound - ing sea. ___   You're high a - bove me now. You're
got ___ to be. ___   You're high a - bove me, fly - ing
sound - ing sea. ___   I feel it in my soul. It's